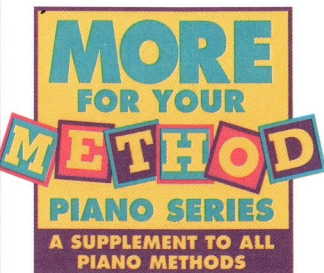

MORE FOR YOUR METHOD PIANO SERIES
A SUPPLEMENT TO ALL PIANO METHODS

Classic Pops

Arranged By Tony Caramia

YO-DDP-615

Hal Leonard's "More For Your Method" series presents your favorite music in arrangements that use only those skills your method book teaches. The key on this page will even tell you at what point in your method you will be ready to play each piece!

After you find the method book you are using, choose the piece you wish to play. Use the key to discover what page in your method you have to complete before you will know everything you need to know to play that piece.

TERRY SNOWDEN PIANO STUDIO
4160 N.E. SANDY BLVD.
PORTLAND, OR 97212

PAGE		Aaron Piano Course 2	Agay Learning To Play Piano 2-3	Alfred Basic Library 3-4	Bastien Piano Lessons 4	Bastien Piano Basics 4	Clark Music Tree C	Gillock Piano All The Way 3-4	Glover-Stewart Method For Piano 3	Noona Basic Piano 6	Olson-Bianchi-Blickenstaff Pathways D	Pace Music For Piano 2-3	Schaum Piano Course C-E	Thompson Piano Course 2
10	I Dreamed A Dream	44	64 (2)	30 (3)	6	6	59	26 (3)	44	47	35	10 (2)	8 (C)	26
8	In The Mood	44	55 (3)	19 (4)	32	30	59	40 (4)	46	47	37	32 (3)	3 (E)	26
4	Spinning Wheel	44	55 (3)	19 (4)	32	30	59	40 (4)	46	47	37	32 (3)	3 (E)	26
2	You've Got A Friend	44	64 (2)	30 (3)	6	6	59	26 (3)	44	47	35	10 (2)	8 (C)	26
14	The Way We Were	44	64 (2)	30 (3)	6	6	59	26 (3)	44	47	35	10 (2)	8 (C)	26
6	Yesterday	44	64 (2)	30 (3)	6	6	59	26 (3)	44	47	35	10 (2)	8 (C)	26

Editor: Barbara Kreader • Transcriber/Arranger: Greg Starr • Cover Illustration: Carol Horzempa

Hal Leonard Publishing Corporation
7777 West Bluemound Road P.O. Box 13819 Milwaukee, WI 53213

YOU'VE GOT A FRIEND

Words and Music by CAROLE KING

Tenderly

With pedal

Lyrics:
When you're down, and trou-bled and you need some love and care, and noth-in', noth-in' is go-in' right.

Close your eyes and think of me and soon I will be there, to bright-en up e-ven your dark-est night.

16
You just call out my name and you know, where-ev-er I
20
am, I'll come run - nin' to see you a -
23
gain.
Win-ter, spring, sum-mer or fall,
26
all you have to do is call, and I'll
29
be there. You've got a friend.

SPINNING WHEEL

Words and Music by DAVID CLAYTON THOMAS

What goes up
You got no money;

must come down.
you got no home.

Spin-ning wheel
Spin-ning wheel,

got to go round.
all a - lone.

Talk-in' 'bout your trou-bles, it's a cry - in' sin.
Talk-in' 'bout your trou-bles, and you nev - er learn.

Ride a paint-ed po-ny, let the spin-ning wheel spin.

Did you find your di-

rect - ing sign on the straight and nar - row high - way.

5

Would you mind a re - flect - ing sign? Just let it shine with -

in your mind, and show you the col - ors that are real.

Some-one is wait-ing just for you.____

Spin-ning wheel, spin-ning true. Drop all your trou-bles by the

riv-er side. Catch a paint-ed po-ny on the spin-ning wheel ride. *ff*

YESTERDAY

Words and Music by
JOHN LENNON and PAUL McCARTNEY

Slowly

Yes - ter - day,
p Sud - den - ly,

all my trou - bles seemed so
I'm not half the man I

With pedal

far a - way.
used to be.

Now it looks as though they're
There's a sha - dow hang - ing

here to stay. Oh
o - ver me. Oh,

I be - lieve in
yes - ter - day came

yes - ter - day.
sud - den - ly.

Why she had to go, I don't know, she would - n't

say.

I said

some - thing wrong, now I

long for yes - ter - day._____

Yes - ter - day,

love was such an eas - y

game to play.

Now I need a place to

hide a - way. Oh,

I be - lieve in

yes - ter - day.

pp Mm - mm - mm - mm - mm - mm - mm._____

IN THE MOOD

Words and Music by JOE GARLAND

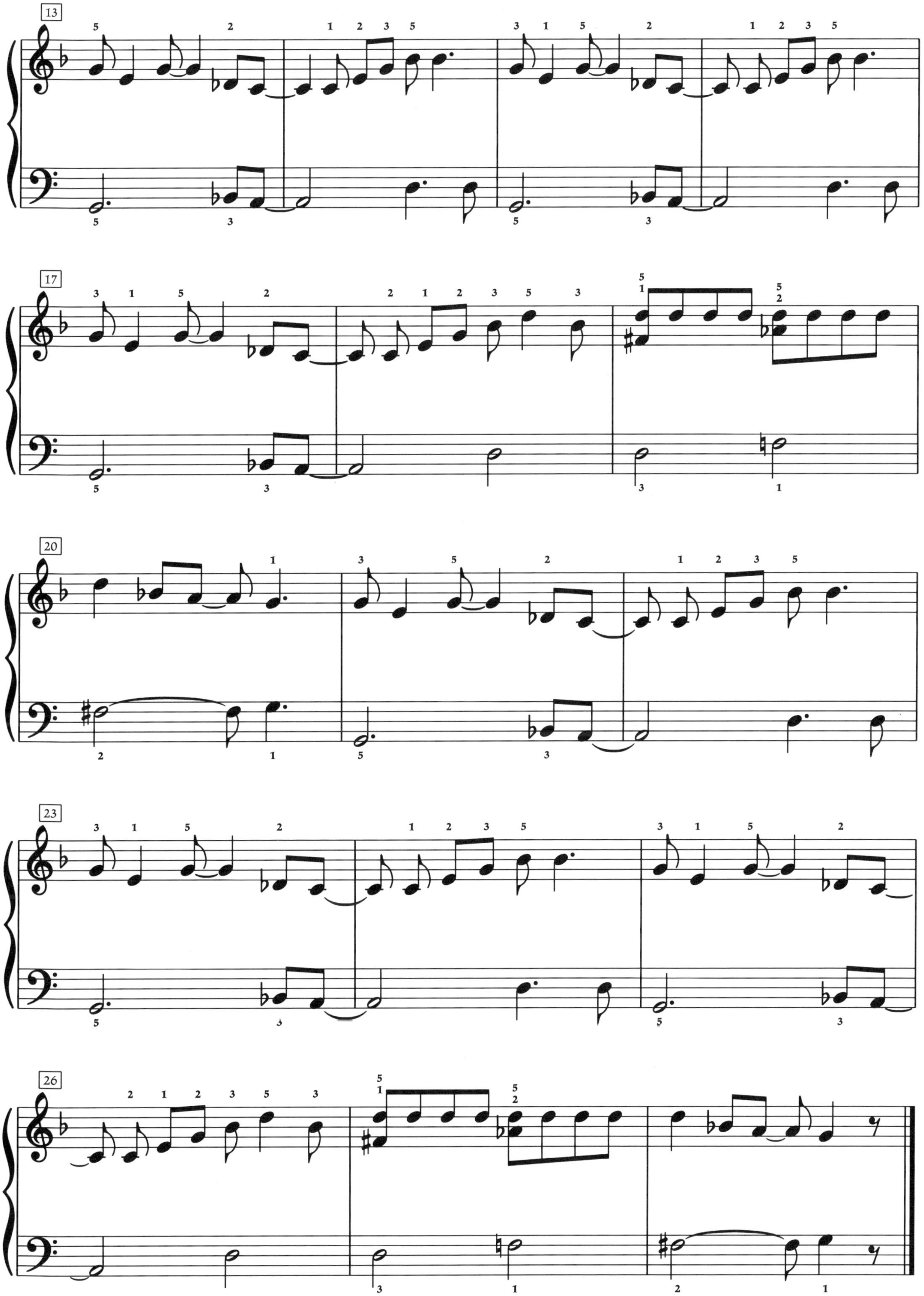
13
17
20
23
26

I DREAMED A DREAM

Lyrics by HERBERT KRETZMER
Original Text by ALAIN BOUBLIL & JEAN-MARC NATEL
Music by CLAUDE-MICHEL SCHONBERG

Reflectively

With pedal

I dreamed a dream in time gone by,

when hope was high and life worth liv - ing.

I dreamed that love would nev - er die.

I dreamed that God would be for - giv - ing. Then, I was young and un - a -

fraid.

And dreams were made and wed and wast-ed.

There was no ran-som to be paid, no song un-sung, no wine un-

tast-ed. But the ti-gers come at night.

with their voi-ces soft as thun-der. As they tear your hope a-

part, As they turn your dreams to shame.

He slept a sum-mer by my side.

He filled my days with end-less won - der.

He took my child-hood in his stride. But he was gone when au-tumn came.

And, still I dream he'll come to me.

That we would live the years to - geth - er.

But there are dreams that can-not be, and there are storms we can-not wea - ther. I had a dream my life would be so dif-f'rent from this hell I'm liv-ing, so dif-f'rent now from what it seemed. How life has killed the dream I dreamed.

rit.

THE WAY WE WERE

Words by ALAN and MARILYN BERGMAN
Music by MARVIN HAMLISCH

Slowly

Mem - 'ries_____ light the cor - ners of my
pic - tures_____ of the smiles we left be -

With pedal

mind.
hind,

Mist - y wa - ter col - or
smiles we gave to one an -

mem - 'ries_____ of the way we were.
oth - er_____ for the way we

Scat - tered were.

11 Can it be that it was all so sim - ple then,

13 or has time re - writ - ten ev - 'ry line?

15 If we had the chance to do it all a - gain, tell me

17 would we? Could we? Mem - 'ries___

20 ___ may be beau - ti - ful, and yet,

what's too pain-ful to re - mem - ber____ we sim-ply choose to for -

get. So it's the laugh - ter,

we will re - mem - ber,____ when-ev - er we re -

mem - ber____ the way we were;

the way we were.